Chimaera

Noelle Cypris

This is for you,
For being everything
You said you were,
And never pretending
To be something else;
For being acquainted
With the war going on
Between my heart and my mind,
And sticking around anyway.

Boss Lady

You can't grasp why

She isn't clinging

To your every word

Or fawning over

Your every move.

What you need

To know about her

Is that

She's independent.

She doesn't need you,

She wants you.

Understand the difference.

The Ugly Truth

Too often,

The people who

Are supposed to love

And support you,

And celebrate your success,

Are the very same people

Who have been praying,

Every night,

For your failure.

Foreshadowing

There's something to be said

About the fact

That when we first started dating,

Someone close to you

Whispered to me,

"He doesn't know how

To be a boyfriend."

I scoffed at that remark.

Because I couldn't foresee

The utter chaos

I would experience

From not heeding

That warning.

Personal Ad

It's gotten to the point

That if you want to find

A genuine person

To spend time with,

You have to add

"Looking for someone

Who is loyal

And not dishonest."

To your dating profile.

Precious Metals

He promises you a life

Of silver and gold,

But you want to tell him

That copper and bronze

Will do just fine,

As long as he

Showers you

With love.

Windy

As I lay here

On the couch,

My heart aching

For you to return,

I hear the wind

Howling outside,

And all I can hope

Is that it's the sound

Of the universe

Blowing you away

From my mind.

Reverse Logic

Why is it that

I have to let you

Fuck me

Before you

Give me the chance

To get to know you

As a person?

When did things become

So backwards?

Hillside

My love,

You are as gorgeous

As the wild grass

On a hillside,

Dancing in the wind

Along a scenic driving route.

Don't let anyone

Mow down your spirit.

Texting

You take the longest time

To reply to my texts,

As if I'm not

Important enough

To acknowledge.

For the record,

If I wanted to wait

For your response,

I would have mailed you

A fucking letter.

Excuses

He gives you excuses

As to why he can't seem

To find the time

To come and see you.

Maybe you should

Start giving him excuses

As to why you can't seem

To care about him

Anymore.

Trophy

If he can't see how lucky he is

To have won your heart,

It's time to let him go.

Because, my love,

You truly are

A prize.

Neediness

It doesn't make you needy

Because you want him

To acknowledge you

As his significant other.

If he doesn't want to claim you,

That's fine.

When he realizes

What he's done

By pushing you away,

It's going to be

The greatest loss

He's ever endured.

Then he'll understand

What true neediness is.

Rest

You've had a rough day,

My dear.

Why don't you

Lay back

And let me

Put your body to work

So that you

Can give your mind

A rest?

Confession

The truth?

I like you.

A lot.

Probably more than I should.

But here's the thing,

You like me too.

And I'm willing to do

Whatever it takes

To keep this spark

Ignited.

Brightness

Your smile outshines

All of the stars

In the night sky

And your eyes

Light up the world

Brighter than the sun

Has ever done.

Knock Knock

I have been begging you

To let me in

Since I first met you,

Yet time and time again,

You keep me locked

Out in the cold.

I'm beginning to see

That maybe some doors

Aren't worth opening.

How To

"What can I do

To make myself

More beautiful?"

You asked me.

Step One: Look in the mirror

Step Two: Smile

Step Three: Repeat

Solar System

You are the sun,

My love,

And I am the planets,

Rotating around you,

Basking in your

Gravitational pull.

Scalpel

You made me

Completely cut

My life apart,

Just to please you,

Then you left me

To bleed out

By myself.

What Happened?

People ask me all the time

What happened to us,

While eying me suspiciously,

As if I have some juicy secret

Hidden in my mind's closet.

And I often wonder

If people look at you

And try to pry into your soul

The same way.

Pressure Cooker

Life-changing events

Were occurring all around us.

I shot you a glance,

As if to pressure you

Into making your big move.

Looking back on it,

That was the worst form

Of peer-pressure

I have ever

Imposed upon anyone.

For that,

I am sorry.

RVIII: Sunnyside Up

I'm sitting on the couch,

Typing away in silence,

And watching you

In the kitchen.

You're clothed

Solely in your boxers,

As you cook us breakfast,

With your back toward me.

I'm sure

You don't even realize

How much peace

And absolute joy

You're bringing

To my world

At this exact moment.

Time Misconception

Everyone is under the impression

That longevity means stability.

I implore you to change

Your mindset on that.

I am in a much happier

And healthier relationship today,

With someone

I've been seeing

For only a short while,

Than I was

With someone I chained myself to

For six years.

The right one is out there

And when you're ready,

Time will bring them to you.

Nudes

If the first thing he asks you,

After a long

And exhausting day,

Is for you to send him

Pictures of your body,

Let him know,

That if he really wants

To see you naked,

He should ask you

What's on your mind.

Falling Star

With all the people

In the world

That you could

Have chosen to

Dive into,

How is it that

I got lucky enough

For you to fall

Into my lap?

Cheers

Darling, this one is for you.

For everything you've done,

And everything you've

Had to suffer through

To get to this amazing point

In your life.

You truly are

Remarkable.

Good Things

They tell me that

Good things come

To those who wait.

So, I've been

Counting down

The days of this year,

Waiting for something positive

To find me.

It looks as though

You've finally arrived.

Returns/Exchanges

Is there any way

I can get a refund

On the time I invested

In trying so hard

To make you and I

Function properly?

Civic I

She was driving.

She saw your leg

Shaking rapidly;

A clear sign

Of anxiety.

"Are you okay?"

She asked, concerned.

Without warning,

You smacked her

Across the face,

So hard,

Her head smashed into

The driver's side window.

It was your harmful reaction

To her harmless question.

Update

"I'm not trying to change you, babe,"

He said, as he took away

The chips she was enjoying

And handed her

A bowl of carrots.

"Look at it as

Getting an update."

"Oh, that's considerate,"

She said thoughtfully,

"As a matter of fact,

I have an update for you:

We're through."

Have Courage

What do you want out of life?

You want to be a pilot?

Learn to fly.

You want to be a body builder?

Train like one.

You want to be an author?

Write your story.

Whatever you want to do,

Have the courage

To believe in yourself

And take the necessary risks

To get it accomplished.

Recovery

I don't know

What struggles

You're going through

At the moment.

What I do know,

Sweetheart,

Is that you are going to rise

From the ashes of this,

And begin again.

Quicksand

I can't put my finger on

What initially drew me to you,

But I've fallen for your laugh,

And the way your face

Looks when you first

Wake up.

I've fallen for how

You rest your head

On my shoulder,

And the way your hand

Fits in mine.

You've sucked me down

Into your pit of quicksand,

And I don't ever want

To come back up.

Cruise Ship

You're under the impression

That because he's not

Returning your love,

You've capsized your ship.

Listen to me, babe,

Focus on loving yourself.

The captain of your seas

Will find you

When you're ready.

Vampiric

You can't have garlic.

You can't have alcohol.

You can't spend too much time

In the sun.

Your body aches and pains,

When everyone else you know

Walks around without

A care in the world.

You rarely complain

About any of this,

Even though you

Have every right to.

Do you understand, my love,

What a uniquely strong

And incredible individual

This makes you?

Self-Doubt

Beautiful girl,

With all of the hardships

That you've had to endure

And that you've risen above,

Why do you still doubt

Your ability to make

Marvelous things happen?

Celestial

She deserves the sun

And if you keep refusing

To give it to her,

Someone else

Will walk into her life

And give her the sun,

Along with the moon

And all of the stars

In the sky.

Dreams

You can laugh at my dreams,

If you must,

And I won't have time

To give a damn.

I'll be too busy

Conjuring up bigger ones,

Without you in them.

Chimaera

You thought you could

Destroy her.

But she was forged together

With the mightiest parts

Of all the most

Magnificent creatures

In the universe.

She is more powerful

Than you ever imagined

She could be.

And you will never

Get the best of her.

Stagnate

Do what your heart desires

And make yourself happy.

If he only wants

To hold you back,

Let him go.

He's not supposed to be

Your anchor.

Hero

Save you?

You don't need anyone

To rescue you from

The tower of troubles

You've been trapped inside.

You're your own hero.

Krispy Kreme

The neon light

Glowed in the window:

HOT DONUTS NOW.

And though I've always

Been fond of deliciously

Glazed pastries,

I decided to go

For something sweeter

In your backseat.

Futuristic

Be with someone

Who doesn't scoff at you

When you tell them

About the future

You can see yourself

Having with them.

Shattered

I am trying to collect

And put back together

The pieces of myself

That you so carelessly smashed

When you decided

I wasn't enough

For you.

Disbelief

"I can't believe you guys

Aren't together anymore.

He was such a nice guy,"

She said, as she

Looked at me accusingly.

And I had to hold my breath

In an attempt

To choke back

The gripping rage I felt

At the fact

That you were so good

At masking your true self

To others.

Proof

They boisterously tell you,

Everyday,

How badly you're going to fail.

Quietly prove them all wrong.

Counterfeit

You were incapable of feeling

Any true emotions.

So, you took a sample of smiles

And a sample of caring

From each person you met,

And you practiced them,

To put on a show

For everyone to see.

My List

Things I lost when you left:

1. Something to warm

    My cold feet at night.

2. Refer to number one.

But now I remember,

There is something

They call blankets.

And since that's the case,

I guess it's safe

To say

I lost nothing.

A La Carte

All along,

I was under the impression

That you were

Going on

Behind my back

With her.

I didn't realize,

Until it was too late,

That I was just

Your appetizer

And she was always

Your main course.

Snooping

I never intended on snooping,

But you were asleep,

And I was in the dark.

I heard the continuous buzz,

And kept seeing

The illumination,

From your phone

On the ceiling.

One glance was all it took,

For me to grasp the truth.

You see,

I never intended on snooping,

But you were asleep,

And I was in the dark.

He Loves Me

I told myself,

As you used your venomous words

To bring me to tears.

He loves me,

I told myself,

As you ignored my calls,

Time and time again.

He loves me,

I told myself,

As I watched you,

From across the bar,

Thinking I was at home,

While you were

Kissing someone else.

He loves me,

Doesn't he?

Beggar

He wants to keep her around

For when he's bored,

But doesn't want to see her

When she needs him most.

Sooner or later,

She's going to wise up,

Because she's tired of trying

To capture his attention,

Unsuccessfully.

She won't beg.

Beacon

Just when I start to think

That the world is a dark

And dreary place,

I find a glimmer of hope

In the light of your soul.

Mended

You kissed my scars

And taught me

That even the most

Shattered of things

Can be reassembled

And come out

Even more beautiful

Than they were before.

Expedition

I've searched,

High and low,

For someone like you.

I've journeyed,

Through hell and back,

And I'll be damned

If I ever let you

Slip out of my grasp.

Hearth

You pull her close,

As you sit together,

In front of the cozy fireplace,

And you take comfort in knowing

That it's your love for each other

That's actually keeping

You both warm.

Rebirth

You tried to drown her

In an ocean of insults

And abuse,

But she held her breath,

And floated

Back to the surface

To start anew.

I guess you forgot

She was indestructible.

Ephemeral

You're the type of person

That one only comes across

Once in a lifetime.

You have a spirit

Containing all the magnificence

Of lightning,

As it flashes across

A darkened sky.

<u>Optimist</u>

Today I want you

To think about all of the

Wonderous things you are,

And not worry about

The things you are not.

Sweater Weather

It's about that time of year,

When you display your

Love for her

By wrapping her in

Your biggest sweater,

And softly kissing her forehead,

Until she falls asleep.

Combat Zone

If I have to fight

For your attention,

With all due respect,

Fuck your attention.

Crosshairs

You have me

Right where

You want me.

The question is,

When are you going to

Pull the trigger?

Shampoo

You hurt me

In the cruelest way

You could think of.

You made an effort

To ensure that I would

Suffer a lifetime

Full of painful

Memories of you.

But I can no longer

Hold on to that trauma.

I have to move on,

And I can't wait to wash

You out of my hair.

No Take-Backs

You push

And you push,

But you can only

Push her away

So many times

Before she decides that

She is no longer

Going to be resistant.

What are you going to do

When it finally hits you

That you'll never

Get her back?

Difficulty

It must be difficult knowing

That if you only loved her

While she still cared about you,

You'd still have her.

Amnesia

I've forgotten

What it was like

To know who I was.

I can't believe

I let you

Change the parts of me

That used to

Matter to me most.

Token

Do you ever

Look at someone

And see your destiny

And your downfall

All in the

Same token?

Pixilated

You told me

You could foresee us,

Walking along the path

Of life together,

Side by side,

Hand in hand.

As beautiful

As your vision sounds,

I just can't seem

To get it

To come into focus.

Undone

Listen my dear,

Every life decision

You've made

Can be undone,

Even the big ones.

You're never stuck.

Try to remember that

When you start to forget

What happiness looks like.

Recognized

I want to be known for

The peace and fulfillment

That I bring to others.

I want to be known for

The good I've done,

And forgiven for the

Negative energy

I've displayed

In times of weakness.

The Gram

Be mindful that

No one is posting

Their failures or misfortunes

Online.

Don't base your life

On somebody else's

Highlight reel.

New Year Pledge

You listened close

As I whined

And complained

About how big of a toll

This year

Had taken on me.

And when I was done,

You took my face

Between your hands,

Looked deep into my eyes,

And said,

"I promise you,

I will make next year

The best year

You've ever had."

Your Type

You're the type of girl

That walks into a lion's den,

With a smile on her face,

And walks away

Without a scratch

On her.

Bed Sheets

When our rendezvous

For the night

Is through,

You always leave the souvenir

Of your scent

On my sheets.

It is a callous reminder

That you've gone,

And a delicious reminder

Of how extraordinary

You make me feel.

Crying

You've been conditioned

To believe that crying

Is a sign of weakness.

That simply isn't the case.

Water is a symbol

Of rebirth,

And your tears

Are your body's way

Of letting you

Start anew.

Grateful

Occasionally,

I still feel

My blood boil

At the thought of

How much

Disorder

You brought

Into my life.

But I also feel

A sense of gratitude

For you,

For teaching me

To put my needs

First.

Fool's Gold

You're the real deal, sweetheart,

But he's too busy

Chasing after these counterfeit types

To appreciate your value.

Standards

You say

My standards are unrealistic

Because I expect

For you

To return my calls

And acknowledge

That I'm yours.

How could I

Have had the audacity

To hold such

High standards?

Hopeless Romantic

Lately,

I can't tell if

I'm a hopeless romantic,

Or just plain hopeless.

Unwanted Attention

How dare you

Assume that just because

She's nice to you,

She should respond

Positively to your

Sexual advances.

She is your friend,

She enjoys your company,

And she does not

Need to feel

Like she owes you

Her body

Just because

You spend a little time

With her.

So What?

"So what

If you think

You're broken?"

He asked her,

"I intend on

Spending an eternity

Helping you put

Your pieces

Back together."

Darkness

If he wants

To keep you

In the dark,

Baby,

He doesn't deserve

To witness

Your glow.

Shower Promises

They stood together

Under the cascading water,

Engulfed in steam.

"Be with me forever,"

He whispered to her.

"That's a long time,"

She said,

"What if you

Change your mind?"

"Impossible,"

He told her,

"I don't believe in breaking

Shower promises."

Civic II

You invited her

To your brother's

Birthday party.

You plied her full of drinks,

To make her more agreeable.

You told her that she

Should sleep with

You and brother

As a birthday gift.

When she said no,

You carried her,

In her intoxicated state,

To her car.

You then drove her

To a random street,

Where you parked,

Took her phone,

Took her money,

And ripped

Her car door handle off.

Then you

Left her,

Passed out,

With the car on,

In the rain,

In the middle of nowhere.

You later justified

All of it

By saying

She was being

Uncooperative.

Recurrent

I thought it was strange

That you suddenly became

More attentive.

I'm glad that lasted

Roughly a week,

Before you got back

To your neglectful ways.

I was starting

To believe that

You cared again.

11:11

Make a wish, sweetheart.

And then harness the power

Of all your worries

And scars from the past,

And make that wish

Come true.

Options

Baby girl,

You have so many

Other options.

Why are you crying

Over someone

Who wouldn't have

The decency

To hand you a tissue

If he saw your tears?

Apologetic

"I'm sorry"

Loses its value

When you say it

Every single day,

But keep indulging

In the same behavior

That caused you

To apologize

In the first place.

Cave Diving

Your eyes

Could brighten

Even the darkest

Of caves.

Flake

You're constantly

Making plans with me,

And then suddenly

Vanishing

At the last minute.

Let me

Make things easier.

I'm forevermore

Unavailable to you.

Shine

I love the way

You shine

When I tell you

How incredibly special

You are.

Just Give

I don't want you

Only when you're

Having a good day.

Give me every frown,

Give me every tear,

Give me every misadventure,

Give me every disappointment,

Give me every panic attack

And give me every fear.

Just make sure

You're giving me you.

Desperately Solo

Please tell me

That I am the only one,

Even if it's not true.

I've decided

I'd rather

Be happy with lies

Than sad with

The truth.

Don't

Don't marry her

Because you think

It's the next step

In your relationship.

Marry her because

You know

That if you can't wake up

Next to her

For the rest of your life,

It would be a life

You would have

Absolutely no business

Being a part of.

Cracked

You assume

You're in too many pieces

For anyone to want you.

Darling,

You're merely cracked,

And you wear it

Extraordinarily well.

Civic III

You called her

And asked her

To pick you up

From work.

You sat in silence

For the entire ride,

And when she pulled her car

Into the driveway

At the front

Of your house,

You asked her

Why she was

Five minutes late.

She tried to explain

That she lost track of time,

And you responded

By wrapping your hands

Around her throat

And squeezing,

While she gasped for air.

It was something

You had done before.

This time, though,

She reached behind her

And pulled the door handle.

She then leaned

Her body weight back,

So that she fell

Out of the car,

And out of your grasp.

That was the very last time

You ever put

Your despicable hands on her.

Flammable

Be with someone

Who sets your soul

On fire.

Turnstile

Stop letting him

Return

After he leaves you

To enter

Someone else.

You're not

His turnstile.

Flashpoint

In the past,

I was never

Able to tell

The precise moment

I fell in love

With someone.

When it comes to you,

However,

I can recall,

Down to the second,

Exactly when it occurred.

I believe that,

In itself,

Has got to mean

Something incredible.

Trifecta

Darling,

Tell me what's on

Your mind,

Touch me tenderly

With your body,

And show me

How to feel

Your soul.

I want to bask in your

Trifecta.

Intentions

It'll be such

A beautiful thing

When he walks

Into your life

And makes you see

That he has only

The purest of intentions

And solely aims

To handle you

With care.

Expectations

At first, I was

A little wary,

Because when you

Entered my life,

I expected nothing,

Yet you made me

Feel everything.

And I keep waiting

For the other

Shoe to drop

But you continuously

Show me

That your feet

Are already

Firmly planted

With me on the ground.

Go Slowly

Take your time

With him,

My dear.

You've never

Had something

Like him before.

Arise

Sweetheart,

You're a rose

Strong enough

To bloom

Through concrete.

He may try

To keep you buried,

But you're too powerful

For his cement.

Roots

Understand that

My roots have

Been planted

In the wrong gardens before.

This time,

I'm hoping

To cultivate something

Worth harvesting.

Be patient with me.

Sandbagging

I'm absolutely positive

We're through.

I'm just waiting

For my heart

To catch up with

My mind

On that.

Detectable

I was here

For you

The whole time,

But you were never

Really looking.

So many times,

I tried to flag you down,

And your eyes

Seemed to gaze

Right past me.

I tried so hard

To make myself

Visible to you

Still, you decided

Not to see me.

Now, it's too late.

Storybook

I was never certain

You were the one,

I was just sure

I wanted to experience

The fairytale ending

That everyone dreams about.

It happened to be my luck

That our story

Was more a tale of horror,

Than a romance novel.

Rumors

The worst part

Of it all

Is the rumors I've heard,

About myself,

From the lips of those

I thought knew me best.

It's difficult to fathom

How appalling an impression

I must have left

On so many people,

To get them to spread

Such horrendous things

About my character.

Lazy Days

I look forward

To the lazy days.

The days where we lay

Entwined in one another,

Scarcely clothed,

As we regale each other

With tales

Of our past

And dreams

Of our future.

Seafaring

The land never asks

For an apology

From the sea

When its

Temperamental waves

Crash against its shore.

I can only hope

That you'll be

As sympathetic with me

On those rare occasions

That my emotions

Cloud my mind

And I start to act

Out of sorts.

No Rights

I believe you

Lost the rights

To casually as me

How my life is going

When you left me here

Struggling to pick myself

Up off the floor.

Stop texting me.

Stop emailing me.

Stop calling me.

Stop asking my friends

And family about my life.

You no longer

Have the right.

Cookie Cutter

I fell hopelessly

In love

With you

Because you weren't

Like anyone else

I had ever met.

Messages

I'm laughing hysterically,

As I read the messages

You keep sending me.

You want to know

What I've been up to

Since you left?

I've been busy

Not giving a shit

That you were ever here.

Beaming

I can't contain

The feeling of pure delight

I feel when I look at you.

You've helped me

Get through

The worst stage

Of my life.

You have been

The silver lining

During my

Stormiest of times.

Worn Out

I know you're exhausted

From tossing and turning,

Throughout the night,

Constantly thinking

About the next thing

That may go wrong.

Relax, baby girl,

All will turn out

As it's supposed to.

You weren't meant

To worry so much.

Leave

She's done

Asking you to stay.

She's realizing

That she's better off

Without all of the

Pain you cause

Each time you

Try to abandon her.

So, go ahead,

For the last time.

And don't let the door

Hit you in the ass

On your way out.

Igloo

You can only

Freeze her out

For so long

Before she starts

To build herself

A shelter

Out of the ice

You provided

And decides she

No longer needs you

To keep her warm.

Wrong Goblet

I chose the cup

That I drank from.

And I would have spent

An eternity trying to

Regurgitate it back up

If you hadn't

Heaved it up

For me.

Stellar

How do you do it?

Make me feel

Like the entire universe

Is in our favor

With just one kiss?

Your Stare

The way you stare

Into my eyes

Makes me see

The forever in us.

It makes me feel

Like I'm the one.

Do-Overs

You won't be able

To get back what you had

In the beginning,

Before the lying

And the cheating.

It's impossible,

Because now you know

How easy it is

For them to step out

On you.

And despite how

Badly you'll want to,

You'll never

Fully trust them again.

One Word

There is nothing more

Insulting than

When you answer

A lengthy text

With one word.

It's the perfect way

To tell someone

You don't give a fuck

About them.

Captured

He's got you trapped

Under his spell.

You know

He's not worth

All the trepidation,

But for some reason

He's got your

Heart in chains

And it's crushing

Your spirit.

Sooner or later

You need to

Start planning

Your escape.

Comforting

You've become

A warm blanket

On the coldest of nights

And a soft pillow

To rest my weary head upon.

You've become

The safest place

I've ever known.

You've become my home.

Repeat Offender

Why do I keep

Allowing you

To build me up,

Just to tear me

Right back down?

I'm so addicted

To the high

You give me,

But the low

Is so damning.

Attention Wasted

Why even text her

In the first place

If you don't truly

Want to hold

A conversation?

There are other people

Who are would love

To have her attention,

And you're

Wasting it.

Greedy

You take and take

From her,

Like a leech

From a swamp.

You use her for

Her body.

You abuse her mind.

You suck every bit

Of peace out of her,

And then you discard her,

Until you need

Sustenance again.

Tell me,

When will

Enough be enough?

Moonlight Sonata

You thought he was everything,

But he constantly made

You feel like

You were nothing.

Baby girl,

He's not the one.

Your true counterpart

Is out there,

Pining for you.

You just have to wait

Until your soul

Is ready to dance

In the moonlight

With his.

Prioritize

I put your needs

Above mine,

Without question.

Yet, when I ask you

For the simple favor,

Of showing up,

When you say you will,

You can't be bothered.

I guess I'm not that high

Of a priority for you.

Courting

You courted her for months.

Made her fall into your clutches

And into your bed.

And when you finally got

What you wanted from her,

You stopped returning her calls.

And a few days later,

You breezed through

The doorway at work

With your wife

And newborn baby,

Between your arms.

Two things you just so happened

To forget to mention

While you were

Between her legs.

Dwelling

I haven't had a home

In a long time.

You being here

Makes it feel

Like a home.

Stay with me.

Hesitation

"So what are you going to do

When I leave?"

He asked her,

"Are you going to

Pursue someone else?"

Without hesitation,

She said,

"Of course I am,

I don't have

Time to waste

Mourning the loss

Of someone

Who was never

Really here."

Schematics

I had every intention

Of drawing you

Into my future,

But when it came down to it,

You didn't make it

Onto my blueprint.

Grave Mistakes

You're in a hole,

And you know

You can't complain

Because you did this

To yourself.

But darling,

Don't come undone

Just yet.

For you can dig

Yourself

Right back out.

You just need

To find

The right shovel.

The Real World

Don't just

Take what you can get.

You can have

Whatever it is

That you desire.

Don't settle for something

Just because

You think that's

What would happen

In the "real world."

Your world

Is the only one

That matters.

Unexpected

It's coming for you.

Whatever it is that you

So desperately want,

And have given up on.

It's going to hit you

Right between those

Big, beautiful eyes

When you least expect it.

Have faith.

Feel It

Be with someone

Who doesn't

Push you away

The moment you express

Your feelings to them.

Privacy

He won't take pictures

With you.

He won't let you post

Anything indicating

You two are together.

He only texts you

On Snapchat, where

Your proof of correspondence

Disappears into thin air.

You feel like he's embarrassed

To admit you exist.

Sweetheart, you must refuse

To be kept hidden

Behind closed doors.

You deserve to be

Shown off to the world.

Flat Earth

If the world was flat,

I'd travel to the edge,

With my hand in yours,

To gaze out at the universe,

And thank it

For bringing you

To me.

Forced

With you,

It was never forced.

Nothing about us

Was plotted or planned.

We spent time together,

Once,

And we both knew,

Without having to say it,

That we would be spending

Most of our time together,

Every day,

After that.

Check-Ups

To the ones

Who check

That everyone else

Is okay

Before they even think

About themselves,

I commend you.

You don't always receive

The gratitude you deserve.

Know that

When the verbal

Recognition is lacking,

Your kind

And caring gestures

Do not go

Unnoticed.

Your Eyes

I know your eyes

Are dancing

Across these pages,

As they fill with tears

From the hurt

And confusion

Consuming your thoughts.

I hope these words

Give you

The comfort you seek

As you try to emerge

From the troubles

Engulfing your mind.

You'll get through this.

Known Facts

I'm not going around

Telling of all

The atrocious things

That you've done.

I just want you to know

That I know.

You were so good

At being so terrible.

Tell me,

Did you have

Yourself fooled

As severely

As you had

Me fooled?

I'm Here

You're not used

To someone caring

So deeply about you,

And you're unsure

How legitimate it is.

Darling, I'm here

To be with you,

And I don't intend on

Going anywhere

Anytime soon.

Let me ease your mind,

And give you

The type of love

You've been

Pining for.

In the Deep

You've got the face

And the body

Of the purest of angels,

But your heart

Is as cold

And dark

As the deepest part

Of the sea.

So Much More

I have fallen for you

Because you are much more

Than just handsome.

You're smart,

You're funny,

And when misfortune befalls you,

You wear a smile on your face,

And keep forging ahead.

I don't know how

You can't see

That you're so much more

Than you let

Yourself believe.

Relics

You look at me

As if you've just

Stumbled across

The most precious

Artifact that your eyes

Have ever

Or will ever

Lay upon again.

You look at me

The way I've been starving

To be looked at

My entire life.

Come True

As if out of thin air,

You galivanted into my life

And showed me that even I

Deserve everything

I've ever dreamt about having.

And you've selflessly brought

To my attention,

That it's you.

You're my living,

Breathing

Dream.

Monstrosity

I thought you were

Hand-sewn together,

Just for me,

But as time went on,

I realized that you were

Carelessly stitched together,

With all of the worst parts

That humanity

Had to offer.

Companion

You're not

Traveling alone

On this road,

I've been with you

Since the start

Of this journey.

And no matter what happens

Along the way,

I'm coming with you.

Latch Key Siblings

When our mother and father

Were busy working

Long hours during the week,

We would come

Home from school

And take care of each other.

On those long afternoons,

We were all we had.

I cherish those memories

And the trouble we got into.

We helped raise each other.

And we did a pretty damn

Good job.

Claimant

I guess what

I'm confused about

Is why I have

To give you

Relationship benefits

When you claim

That we're not

In a relationship.

Confidential

Beautiful girl,

You are not

His secret case file.

You were never meant

To be kept

Confidential.

Waiting Room

You don't have

To sit at home,

Sad and lonely,

Awaiting his return,

When he goes out.

Enjoy yourself.

If he doesn't want

That for you,

Then he doesn't

Get to have you.

Garbage Men

There are men who will use you.

There are men who will ignore you.

There are men who will act as if

They want to give you the world

On a silver platter,

But instead all they give you

Is sorrow and betrayal.

There are men that will leave you

Starving for attention,

While driving you

To the brink off insanity

Questioning what

You're doing wrong.

These types of men exist

As lessons.

But not every lesson

Is one you should master.

You will find a deep love,

One that is worthy of

Your time and energy,

But you must first learn

To stop digging

Through the trash

When you're looking for

A treasure.

Horoscope

My favorite time at night

Has become

When our eyelids

Are so heavy, we can barely

Keep them open,

And just before we drift off,

Into the day's end,

You nudge me to remind me

That we must find out

What the stars have in store

For us tomorrow.

No New Messages

Sending and receiving emails

Started seeming to me

Like a primitive form

Of communication.

But then I met you,

And even though

You're busy,

You send me emails

While you're

Engulfed in work,

Just to see how my day

Is going.

And now the most

Disappointing sentence to me

Has become the one that says:

No new messages.

Stunning

You brought me to

The top of a mountain

To show me

What you called,

"The most amazing view

I would ever see."

But my knees

Were weak

And my head was light

From having travelled

To the top

Alongside the most

Stunning person

My eyes had ever had

The pleasure of seeing.

Auto-Correct

She will survive,

And recover,

But she will never

Be the same.

You can't truly believe

That the awful things

You've put her through

Will just fix themselves.

There is no auto-correct

For real life.

Luminous

You shy away from me

When you feel

Like you're showing me

Too much

Of your

Self-proclaimed

Dark side.

That's unnecessary,

My love.

I have enough light

For the both of us.

Effervescent

As much as

I'd like to

Conceal it,

You can plainly see

That my feelings

For you

Are bubbling over

Like a freshly popped

Bottle of champagne.

Please,

Be careful with them.

Closing

I'll try to let them go;

The things you've done,

The havoc you've wreaked

Upon my life,

In an attempt

To tear my whole world

Apart.

You have no place

In my future.

And I pray that someday,

I forget

The role you played

In my past.

Chimaera

Want to read more?

Check out another work by Noelle Cypris:

Blenderhead

Available now!

Made in the USA
Columbia, SC
23 November 2018